Symbols, Landmarks, and Monuments

The
Alamo

Tamara L. Britton
ABDO Publishing Company

visit us at
www.abdopub.com

Published by ABDO Publishing Company, 4940 Viking Drive, Edina, Minnesota 55435.
Copyright © 2004 by Abdo Consulting Group, Inc. International copyrights reserved in
all countries. No part of this book may be reproduced in any form without written
permission from the publisher.

Printed in the United States.

Cover Photo: Corbis
Interior Photos: AP/Wide World pp. 11, 29; Corbis pp. 1, 5, 6-7, 8, 9, 15, 18, 19, 20, 21,
    23, 24, 25, 27, 28, 31

Series Coordinator: Kristin Van Cleaf
Editors: Kate A. Conley, Stephanie Hedlund
Art Direction & Maps: Neil Klinepier

Library of Congress Cataloging-in-Publication Data

Britton, Tamara L., 1963-
    The Alamo / Tamara L. Britton.
        p. cm. -- (Symbols, landmarks, and monuments)
    Includes index.
    Summary: Presents information on the history of the Alamo, including the famous
battle of 1836 that took place there, some of the men involved in that battle, and its
significance in the struggle for Texas's independence from Mexico.
    ISBN 1-59197-518-2
    1. Alamo (San Antonio, Tex.)--Siege, 1836--Juvenile literature. [1. Alamo (San
Antonio, Tex.)--Siege, 1836. 2. Alamo (San Antonio, Tex.) 3. National
monuments.] I. Title.

F390.B845 2003
976.4'03--dc22

                                                                    2003052306

Contents

The Alamo

In San Antonio, Texas, lie the remains of an old Spanish **mission**. It is called the Alamo. Heroic men fought a battle there in 1836. This battle was part of Texas's fight for independence from Mexico.

Since that time, the Alamo has become a symbol of the spirit of the Texas Revolution. During this conflict, many men sacrificed their lives to help free Texas. Soon, it became an independent nation. Later, it became part of the United States.

Every year, many people visit the Alamo. They come to see the place where brave men faced overwhelming odds. Visitors learn how those same men stood their ground to fight for what they believed in.

The Alamo chapel today

Fast Facts

√ The cornerstone of the current chapel was laid on May 8, 1744.

√ The name "Alamo" may have come from the cottonwood trees around the church, known as *álamo* in Spanish.

√ Another theory for the name "Alamo" is that it came from La Compañía de Alamo de Parras, the company of Spanish soldiers who occupied the mission.

√ Santa Anna's siege of the Alamo lasted for 13 days.

√ At least 15 people survived the Battle of the Alamo. One was William B. Travis's slave, Joe. Two others were Susanna and Angelina Dickinson, wife and daughter of a soldier. Other survivors were pro-Texan Mexican women and children.

√ The famous arched front of the Alamo chapel was added by the U.S. Army when it occupied the buildings around 1850.

√ Adina de Zavala and Clara Driscoll both fought to preserve the Alamo as a historical site.

√ The chapel is the only original building of the Alamo still standing.

Timeline

<u>1718</u>	√	Mission San Antonio de Valero was established.
<u>1793</u>	√	The friars abandoned the mission.
<u>1803</u>	√	Spanish soldiers occupied the Alamo.
<u>December 1835</u>	√	Texans took control of San Antonio and the Alamo.
<u>January 19, 1836</u>	√	Colonel James Bowie arrived to investigate the military situation for Governor Henry Smith and General Sam Houston.
<u>February 2, 1836</u>	√	Bowie decided to stay and defend the Alamo; Lieutenant Colonel William B. Travis arrived with 30 men.
<u>February 8, 1836</u>	√	Davy Crockett arrived in San Antonio with 12 volunteers.
<u>February 23, 1836</u>	√	Antonio López de Santa Anna and his forces arrived, beginning the siege of the Alamo.
<u>March 6, 1836</u>	√	The Alamo fell in an early morning attack.
<u>1850</u>	√	The U.S. Army occupied and rebuilt the Alamo.
<u>1880s</u>	√	The Long Barracks were a department store.
<u>1905</u>	√	The Daughters of the Republic of Texas took over the Alamo and made it into a museum.

A Spanish Mission

In 1718, **Franciscan** missionaries built a **mission** in present-day Texas, a region in the colony called New Spain. It was called Mission San Antonio de Valero. The missionaries planned to convert the neighboring natives to Christianity.

The friars abandoned the mission in 1793. Starting in about 1803, Spanish soldiers used it as a military fort. They called it the Alamo. It continued to be used as a fort before becoming a part of Texan history.

Spanish missionaries built missions all over New Spain, such as this one that still stands in San Antonio, Texas.

In early 1821, Moses Austin received a grant from the Spanish government to start a colony in Texas. But, he died before he could begin the settlement. So his son, Stephen F. Austin, took over the grant.

Spanish missionaries perform a religious ceremony at the Alamo chapel. Native people watch, some kneeling and praying.

Stephen F. Austin

Stephen F. Austin was born in Virginia in 1793. When he was five years old, his family moved to Missouri. Austin was elected to the Missouri Territory's legislature in 1814. He also served in the **militia**.

In 1821, Mexico gained its independence from Spain. This new government allowed Austin to keep the grant he had inherited from his father. He led a group of settlers to found a colony in that same year. In time, thousands of Americans came to settle in Texas.

In 1833, Austin went to Mexico City to ask for reforms from the government. But, Mexican officials worried he was plotting a **rebellion**. So on his way back to Texas, he was arrested and sent to prison.

Austin returned to Texas in 1835 and joined the growing rebellion. When the Texas Revolution began, Austin led forces against the Mexican army in San Antonio.

In November 1835, the revolutionary government sent Austin to the United States. His task was to ask for aid and volunteers to help Texas gain independence.

When Austin returned in 1836, Texas was an independent nation. He ran for president in the first election but lost to Sam Houston. Instead, Austin became the nation's first **secretary of state**. He died in Texas in 1836.

This statue of Stephen F. Austin stands above his grave in Austin, Texas.

Rebellion!

In 1821, New Spain received independence from Spain and became Mexico. In 1824, the new **constitution** created the state of Coahuila y Tejas. Part of it included the area called Texas. By 1835, more than 20,000 people had settled there. Most of these colonists were from the United States.

About this time, the United States wanted to buy Texas from Mexico. It had been trying to claim the region for a number of years. However, the Mexican government would not sell it.

At the same time, the Texan colonists wanted independence from Mexico. They thought a law limiting **immigration** from the United States was unfair. Texans also believed the new president, Antonio López de Santa Anna, did not follow the constitution.

In 1835, Texans revolted against Mexico and formed a temporary government. Mexico's army moved in to stop the

rebellion. It claimed the Alamo as its military headquarters.
The soldiers prepared to defend the Mexican **Republic** against
the Texan rebels.

Late in 1835, the Texans fought the Mexicans and captured
the Alamo. So, Antonio López de Santa Anna came to San
Antonio. His goal was to defeat the rebellious Texans.

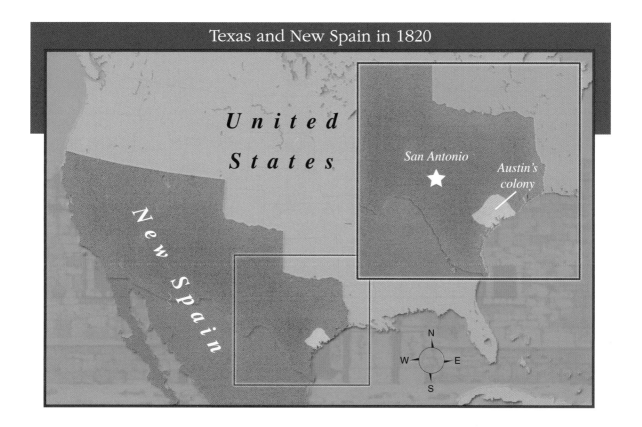

Texas and New Spain in 1820

Antonio López de Santa Anna

Antonio López de Santa Anna was born in Jalapa, Mexico, in 1794. He joined the army when he was just 16 years old. The young soldier moved up the ranks quickly. He became a captain and soon a lieutenant colonel. Later, he was promoted to brigadier general.

In 1833, Santa Anna was elected Mexico's president. He was a strict leader. In fact, he ruled as a **dictator**. Santa Anna quickly defeated those who challenged his power.

Santa Anna served in Mexico's government and military for many years. In 1847, he fought against future president Zachary Taylor at the Battle of Buena Vista. He served as Mexico's president twice more, but he was later overthrown and exiled. He died in Mexico City in 1876.

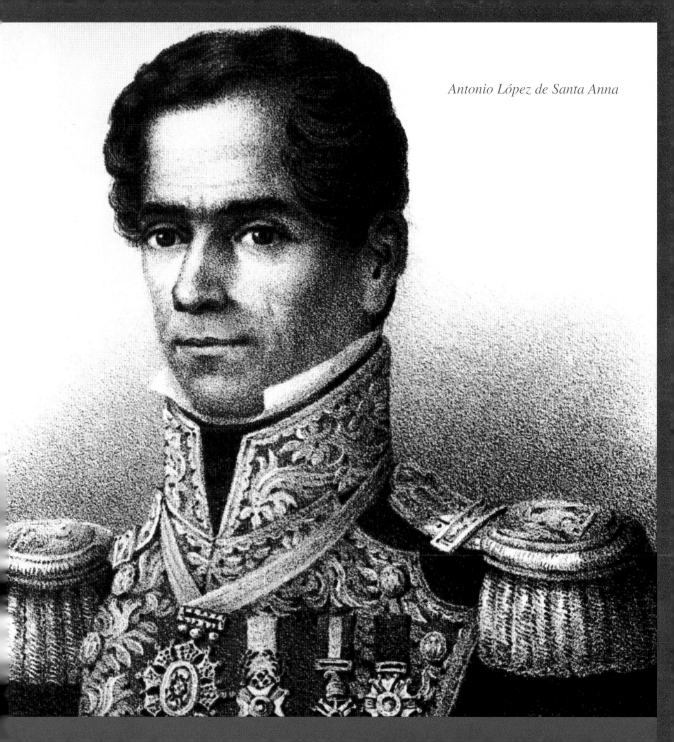
Antonio López de Santa Anna

Digging In

As the **rebellion** began, troops began reinforcing the Alamo. On January 19, James Bowie arrived with a group of volunteer fighters. Lieutenant Colonel William B. Travis arrived on February 2 with more soldiers. Davy Crockett and other volunteers arrived six days later.

Meanwhile, Santa Anna was determined to stop the rebellion. He arrived in San Antonio on February 23, 1836. He and his soldiers quickly defeated Texan troops as they moved toward the Alamo.

Santa Anna and his troops surrounded the Alamo. He called for the Texans' surrender. Colonel Travis refused and fired a cannon. The Alamo came under siege, and Travis sent for help in defending the Alamo.

On March 2, the Texans declared independence. The temporary government drafted a **constitution**. The Texans prepared for a fight.

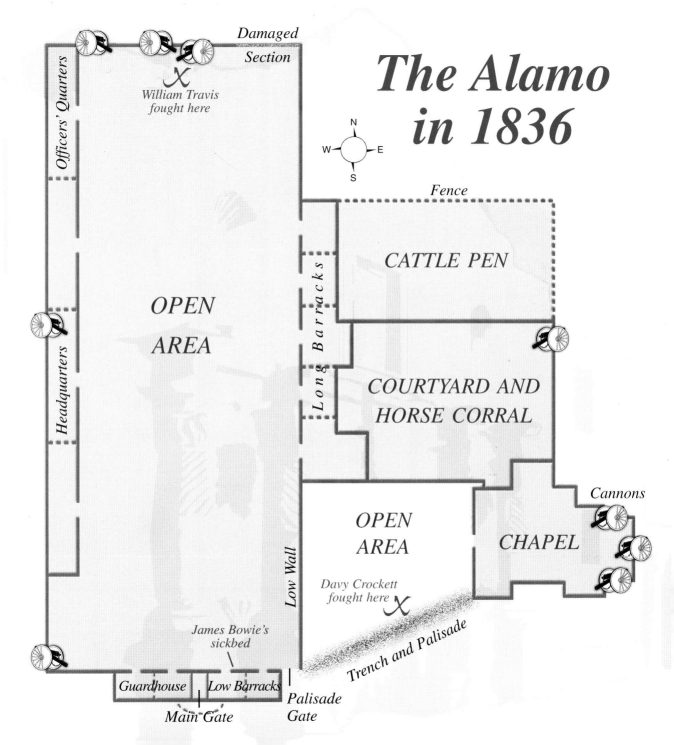

The Alamo in 1836

Officers' Quarters

Damaged Section

X
William Travis fought here

N W E S

Headquarters

OPEN AREA

Fence

CATTLE PEN

Long Barracks

COURTYARD AND HORSE CORRAL

Cannons

CHAPEL

Low Wall

OPEN AREA

Davy Crockett fought here X

Trench and Palisade

James Bowie's sickbed

Guardhouse

Low Barracks

Main Gate

Palisade Gate

William B. Travis and James Bowie

William B. Travis was born in South Carolina in 1809. Eventually, he became a lawyer. Travis moved to Texas in 1831. In 1836, he went to San Antonio to help reinforce the Alamo. There, Travis was put in command of the regular army.

An army of volunteers also fought at the Alamo. They were led by James Bowie. Bowie was born in Kentucky in 1796. In 1802, his family moved to Louisiana.

A statue of William B. Travis on the Alamo memorial

As a young man, Bowie was a lumber trader. In 1828, he moved to Texas and settled in San Antonio. Bowie became a citizen of Mexico two years later. He received land from the Mexican government.

Before the battle for the Alamo began, Bowie took command of the Texans who had volunteered. Unfortunately, he soon became very ill. Bowie fought bravely in the battle for as long as he could, but Travis soon took over command of the volunteers.

James Bowie

Battle for the Alamo

Thirty-two men answered Colonel Travis's call for help. This meant there were now more than 180 men defending the Alamo, and Texas. Outside the Alamo's walls, 5,000 Mexican soldiers were ready to fight.

Travis knew the odds were against them. An Alamo legend says that on March 5, he gathered his men together and drew his sword. With its tip, he drew a line in the dirt.

The defenders cross over Travis's line to stay and defend the Alamo.

Mexican troops attack the Alamo.

Travis said any man who wished to defend the Alamo should cross the line. Although very ill, James Bowie asked for help crossing the line. Davy Crockett also stepped across.

In the end, only one man did not cross the line. Whether or not this story is true, many people tell it as an example of the defenders' courage.

On March 6, Santa Anna gave orders to attack. Mexican troops charged and soon scaled the walls of the fort. Inside, the men fought hand to hand. The Mexicans, who had more soldiers, quickly overcame the Texans.

All of the Alamo's defenders were killed. However, they had made a courageous effort to defend the fort. Mexico's army suffered about 600 **casualties**. But, some say that as many as 1,500 Mexican soldiers may have been killed.

Davy Crockett

Davy Crockett was born in Tennessee in 1786. As a boy, he worked on his family's farm. In 1813, he volunteered for the army and served in the Creek War. He served under future president Andrew Jackson.

In 1821, Crockett was elected to the Tennessee state legislature. He was re-elected in 1823. He ran for a seat in Congress in 1825 but lost. Two years later, he was elected to the House of Representatives. He served two terms.

Crockett lost his next re-election. But, he returned to Congress in 1833 and served two more years. After this term, he was not re-elected.

After losing the re-election, Crockett went to Texas. He joined a group of men who wanted to help Texas gain independence. He went to San Antonio in February 1836. There, he joined the brave men who defended the Alamo.

Davy Crockett

Remember the Alamo!

Santa Anna quickly led 600 to 700 men after the Texan army. On April 20, Santa Anna's men made camp along the San Jacinto River. Early the next day, more troops arrived. Santa Anna then had about 1,300 soldiers under his command.

Late that afternoon, the Mexican soldiers lay down for a rest. General Sam Houston and his troops used the opportunity to attack. The Texan soldiers told each other to "Remember the Alamo!" This gave them the strength and desire to defeat the Mexican troops.

Texas's current flag was also the third flag of the Republic of Texas.

Though Houston's force was only 800 men strong, it was able to kill more than 630 Mexicans. More than 700 were captured. The next day, the troops captured Santa Anna.

Santa Anna agreed to a treaty that would recognize Texas's independence. In October 1836, the **Republic** of Texas set up a permanent government. Sam Houston became the nation's first president.

During the next few years, the young nation struggled. It had little money, and politicians often disagreed on how to run the government. On December 29, 1845, Texas joined the United States as the twenty-eighth state. It is the only state that was once an independent nation.

Texans bring Santa Anna to meet with the wounded Sam Houston.

Sam Houston

Sam Houston was born in Virginia in 1793. In 1807, his family moved to Tennessee. For a time, he lived with a band of Cherokee Native Americans. He later became a schoolteacher.

In 1813, Houston joined the army. He fought at the Battle of Horseshoe Bend with future president Andrew Jackson. He left the army five years later.

Houston studied law and was elected Tennessee's district attorney. In 1823, he was elected to Congress and served two terms. In 1827, he was elected Tennessee's governor. He quit the office two years later.

In about 1832, Houston moved to Texas. He became commander of Texas's army in 1835. The next year, Houston was elected the first president of the independent **Republic** of Texas.

When Texas was admitted to the United States, Sam Houston was one of the state's first two senators. He also served as governor. He died in 1863.

Sam Houston

Symbol of Texas

Since 1836, the Alamo has undergone a number of changes. A few months after the battle, most of the fort was torn down. Only the church, sections of walls, and part of the Long Barracks remained.

The memorial in front of the Alamo includes statues of the defenders.

The Alamo lay in ruins for a number of years. Around 1850, the U.S. Army rebuilt it and used it for a headquarters until 1878. Next, the Long Barracks became part of a department store.

In 1905, the Daughters of the **Republic** of Texas took charge of the Alamo. This group is made up of **descendants** of those who fought for Texas's independence. The Daughters maintain the Alamo as a museum.

Actors pause for a moment of silence before re-enacting the Battle of the Alamo.

Some parts of the Alamo, such as the Long Barracks, have been reconstructed. But, the only original part of the Alamo that remains is the chapel building. A monument at the site lists the names of the brave defenders.

Today, the Alamo is known as the "Cradle of Texas Liberty." It is a memorial to the brave men who fought to help bring independence to Texas. The Alamo is a symbol of their courage, sacrifice, and honor.

Glossary

casualty - a military person lost through death, wounds, or capture.

constitution - the laws that govern a country.

descendant - a person who comes from a particular ancestor or group of ancestors.

dictator - a ruler with complete control who often governs in a cruel or unfair way.

Franciscan - a member of the Order of Friars Minor who is dedicated to preaching, missions, and charities.

immigration - entry into another country to live.

militia - a group of citizens trained for war or emergency.

mission - a center or headquarters for religious work.

rebellion - an armed resistance or defiance of a government.

republic - a form of government in which authority rests with voting citizens and is carried out by elected officials, such as those in a parliament.

secretary of state - a member of the president's cabinet who handles relations with other countries.

Web Sites

To learn more about the Alamo, visit ABDO Publishing Company on the World Wide Web at **www.abdopub.com**. Web sites about the Alamo are featured on our Book Links page. These links are routinely monitored and updated to provide the most current information available.

The Long Barracks

Index